Instant Getting Started with VMware Fusion

Learn everything you need to know to get started with VMware Fusion

Michael Roy

PUBLISHING

BIRMINGHAM - MUMBAI

Instant Getting Started with VMware Fusion

First published: February 2014

Production Reference: 1210214

Published by Packt Publishing Ltd.
Livery Place
35 Livery Street
Birmingham B3 2PB, UK.

ISBN 978-1-78217-788-3

www.packtpub.com

Credits

Author

Michael Roy

Reviewers

Ryan Johnson

Mario Russo

Acquisition Editors

Sam Birch

Subho Gupta

Content Development Editor

Neil Alexander

Technical Editor

Manan Badani

Copy Editor

Laxmi Subramanian

Project Coordinator

Sanket Deshmukh

Proofreaders

Ameesha Green

Paul Hindle

Production Coordinator

Pooja Chiplunkar

Cover Work

Pooja Chiplunkar

Cover Image

Ronak Dhruv

Foreword

The essence of VMware Fusion is to empower people to do incredible things with their Mac. Michael's guide distills years of experience and insights into this practical book so as to get more work done using VMware Fusion Microsoft Windows and the Mac.

Simon Bennett
Product Manager, VMware

About the Author

Michael Roy is a virtualization expert working for VMware, the world's leading virtualization and cloud computing company used by 95 percent of Fortune 500 companies to manage and virtualize their data center infrastructure.

He currently specializes in technical marketing for hybrid cloud services, but started at VMware working on VMware Fusion 2 in 2009 where he co-led a world-class global support team, giving customers the help they needed to get the most out of VMware Fusion.

Prior to VMware, he managed a small data center in downtown Toronto as the senior systems administrator, and also spent two years working for Apple where he became a Mac expert.

When not working with computers, clouds, or virtual machines, he likes to snowboard, surf, and cook, and listen to, play, and create music. Michael's success story at VMware can be found at `http://www.vmware.com/go/mikeroy-journey`.

Firstly, I want to thank VMware for giving me the opportunity of a lifetime. I also want to thank Eric Moore, Ben Gertzfield, Eric Tung, Simon Bennett, Jason Joel, Mike Udaltsov, and the rest of the Fusion support and engineering folks for building and supporting an amazing product and an equally amazing team of people around it. I would finally like to thank my wife, Suzy, for putting up with me during this crazy time of growth.

About the Reviewers

Ryan Johnson is a staff technical account manager, who works for VMware as a part of professional services. He has over 18 years of enterprise experience, including engineering, research and development, enterprise technology and business architecture, service management, and professional services.

Prior to joining VMware, he was the enterprise technology architect for Citizens Property Insurance Corporation of Florida, where he led the Enterprise Architecture Program and was responsible for the aspects of technology, applications, and information architecture.

He holds numerous industry certifications from VMware, Microsoft, EMC, Red Hat, and others.

For a mix of hypertext fragments, pixels, and all things under-analyzed, follow him on Twitter (@tenthirtyam) or on LinkedIn (linkedin.com/in/tenthirtyam).

Mario Russo has worked as an IT architect, a senior technical VMware trainer, and has worked in the pre-sales department. He has also worked on VMware technology since 2004.

In 2005, he worked for IBM on the first large project consolidation for Telecom Italia on the Virtual VMware ESX 2.5.1 platform in Italy with Physical to Virtual (P2V) tool. In 2007, he conducted a drafting course and training for BancoPosta, Italy, and project disaster and recovery (DR Open) for IBM and EMC. In 2008, he worked for the project Speed Up Consolidation BNP and he worked for the migration of P2V on VI3 infrastructure at BNP Cardif Insurance.

He is a VCI Certified Instructor Level 2 of VMware and is certified in VCAP5-DCA. He is the owner of Business to Virtual, which specializes in virtualization solutions.

He was also the technical reviewer of the following *Packt Publishing* books:

▸ *Implementing VMware Horizon View 5.2*

▸ *Implementing VMware vCenter Server*

▸ *Troubleshooting vSphere Storage*

▸ *VMware Horizon View 5.3 Design Patterns and Best Practices*

I would like to thank my wife Lina and my daughter Gaia.
They're my strength.

www.PacktPub.com

Support files, eBooks, discount offers, and more

You might want to visit www.PacktPub.com for support files and downloads related to your book.

Did you know that Packt offers eBook versions of every book published, with PDF and ePub files available? You can upgrade to the eBook version at www.PacktPub.com and as a print book customer, you are entitled to a discount on the eBook copy. Get in touch with us at service@packtpub.com for more details.

At www.PacktPub.com, you can also read a collection of free technical articles, sign up for a range of free newsletters and receive exclusive discounts and offers on Packt books and eBooks.

http://PacktLib.PacktPub.com

Do you need instant solutions to your IT questions? PacktLib is Packt's online digital book library. Here, you can access, read and search across Packt's entire library of books.

Why subscribe?

- ▸ Fully searchable across every book published by Packt
- ▸ Copy and paste, print and bookmark content
- ▸ On demand and accessible via web browser

Free access for Packt account holders

If you have an account with Packt at www.PacktPub.com, you can use this to access PacktLib today and view nine entirely free books. Simply use your login credentials for immediate access.

Instant updates on new Packt books

Get notified! Find out when new books are published by following @PacktEnterprise on Twitter, or the *Packt Enterprise* Facebook page.

Table of Contents

Preface   1

Instant Getting Started with VMware Fusion   5

Installing Windows 7 and upgrading to Windows 8 (Simple)   7

Keeping your old PC alive! (Intermediate)   18

Much ado about snapshots (Intermediate)   21

Keeping Your VM and Your Data safe (Simple)   29

Printing from Windows – how easy it is! (Simple)   33

Network adapters – what's the difference? (Simple)   37

Connecting peripherals to Windows – bringing the outside world in! (Simple)   44

Dedicating an external keyboard exclusively to Windows (Advanced)   46

"I'm stuck, now what?" (Simple)   49

Summary   49

Preface

Welcome to *Instant Getting Started with VMware Fusion*. In this short e-book, we'll get up-to-date with what's new in VMware Fusion 5, and learn how to install Windows 8 or 8.1 as a virtual machine in just a few steps. We'll not only explore how to migrate your existing PC and applications, but also how to manage backups and ensure the security of your virtual machines. Finally, we'll even learn about some new advanced features in Fusion Professional Edition, and how to get help when you need it.

What this book covers

Installing Windows 7 and upgrading to Windows 8 (Simple), demonstrates how to install Windows 8 as a new virtual machine. We'll illustrate the process of using a Windows 7 trial download and upgrading it to a fully licensed copy of Windows 8, and even upgrading it to 8.1. We'll also touch on the role of VMware Tools and also how and when to install it. We'll also show you how to plan ahead to run both Windows 7 and Windows 8 at the same time using snapshots, or linked clones with Fusion 6 Professional.

Keeping your old PC alive! (Intermediate), shows you the steps to make a complete clone of your existing PC in VMware Fusion, and discusses some of the things to consider when doing this.

Much ado about snapshots (Intermediate), shows you VMware Fusion's amazing feature called snapshots, which allows you to roll the virtual machine back in time. We'll show you how to use this to make one virtual machine with both Windows 7 and Windows 8. Pretty cool right?

Keeping Your VM and Your Data safe (Simple), shows you that VMware Fusion does not come with a backup utility, so it's in the hands of users to manage their backups effectively. Here, we'll discuss considerations that should be made when taking backups, how Time Machine can get in the way and how to avoid problems with it, and how to use and manage snapshots. Finally, we'll show you how you can encrypt your virtual machines to increase the security of your virtual machine.

Printing from Windows – how easy it is! (Simple), shows that printing through a virtual machine on Mac is not always a straightforward process. This recipe shows you multiple ways to perform the task with ease.

Network adapters – what's the difference? (Simple), shows you how VMware has developed a virtual network adapter, which allows users to customize the networks in their virtual machines to a greater extent. This recipe shows you how to use it.

Connecting peripherals to Windows – bringing the outside world in! (Simple), teaches you to use the USB pass-through to connect almost any USB device that the Mac detects to your virtual machine.

Dedicating an external keyboard exclusively to Windows (Advanced), extends on the previous one, teaching you how to connect an external keyboard to your computer that can be used exclusively for controlling Windows within the virtual machine.

"I'm stuck, now what?" (Simple), explains where to get more information on VMware Fusion, where to go when you need help, and how to connect with a whole community of VMware Fusion users.

What you need for this book

To complete the tasks outlined in this book, you'll need the following:

▶ An Apple Macintosh computer with VMware Fusion 6 installed

▶ 4 GB of RAM (8 GB or more is recommended for best performance)

▶ 35 GB of hard disk space to complete the installation alone

▶ A recommended 50 GB of free space to accommodate the VM's natural growth

▶ Valid licenses and operating system installation media (disk or disk image) for Windows 7 and/or Windows 8/8.1

Who this book is for

If you are new to the Mac platform but still need to use Windows, or if you are a long-time Mac user who needs multiple operating systems for development or testing, then this is the book for you. If you are a beginner, you will benefit from an explanation on how to make things perform well, and if you are an advanced user, you will learn some interesting tricks that will help you get the most out of your virtual machines.

Conventions

In this book, you will find a number of styles of text that distinguish between different kinds of information. Here are some examples of these styles, and an explanation of their meaning.

A block of code is set as follows:

```
usb.generic.allowHID = "TRUE"
usb.generic.allowLastHID = "TRUE"
```

New terms and **important words** are shown in bold. Words that you see on the screen, in menus or dialog boxes for example, appear in the text like this: "clicking on the **Next** button moves you to the next screen."

 Warnings or important notes appear in a box like this.

In some screens, I use **Text Only** in the toolbar to save space. You can enable this by right-clicking on the toolbar in your **Fusion** window (where you see the **Suspend**, **Snapshots,** and **Devices** icons) and select **Text Only**.

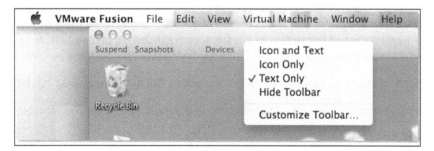

Reader feedback

Feedback from our readers is always welcome. Let us know what you think about this book—what you liked or may have disliked. Reader feedback is important for us to develop titles that you really get the most out of.

To send us general feedback, simply send an e-mail to feedback@packtpub.com, and mention the book title via the subject of your message.

If there is a topic that you have expertise in and you are interested in either writing or contributing to a book, see our author guide on www.packtpub.com/authors.

Customer support

Now that you are the proud owner of a Packt Publishing book, we have a number of things to help you to get the most from your purchase.

Errata

Although we have taken every care to ensure the accuracy of our content, mistakes do happen. If you find a mistake in one of our books—maybe a mistake in the text or the code—we would be grateful if you would report this to us. By doing so, you can save other readers from frustration and help us improve subsequent versions of this book. If you find any errata, please report them by visiting http://www.packtpub.com/submit-errata, selecting your book, clicking on the **errata submission form** link, and entering the details of your errata. Once your errata are verified, your submission will be accepted and the errata will be uploaded on our website, or added to any list of existing errata, under the Errata section of that title. Any existing errata can be viewed by selecting your title from http://www.packtpub.com/support.

Piracy

Piracy of copyright material on the Internet is an ongoing problem across all media. At Packt Publishing, we take the protection of our copyright and licenses very seriously. If you come across any illegal copies of our works, in any form, on the Internet, please provide us with the location address or website name immediately so that we can pursue a remedy.

Please contact us at copyright@packtpub.com with a link to the suspected pirated material.

We appreciate your help in protecting our authors, and our ability to bring you valuable content.

Questions

You can contact us at questions@packtpub.com if you are having a problem with any aspect of the book, and we will do our best to address it.

Instant Getting Started with VMware Fusion

Getting my first Mac was one of the most exciting and personally profound changes I had made in my computing experience. Back in October 2006, I got a MacBook Pro, and it changed my life. No longer did I have to fight with viruses to the same degree and OS X, now finally running on Intel, opened up the possibilities of Boot Camp and installing Windows on a partition, or running multiple operating systems on it through a technology called **virtualization**. So, I could still use Windows if I needed to, but I had the added bonus of a host system that I could trust.

An early problem I had was that I still needed to use some Windows-based apps for work. To solve this, now that Apple had switched to Intel, I started looking into virtualization, and I found a few players on the market. One of them I found to be slow on my MacBook Pro, and while it generally worked, it was pretty buggy and crashed often when I was in the middle of something. Sometime early in 2007, I came upon a beta invitation for a pre-release version of this feature called **Fusion**, from a software company called VMware. I had used **VMware Workstation** for Windows and that already worked well, so I signed up and tried out VMware Fusion. I haven't looked back since.

While Version 5.0 was a far cry from today's Fusion, it was still impressive to have a tool that just worked and allowed me to run Windows and Linux on my new MacBook Pro. With the success of this technology, it no longer matters what platform or operating system we have; now we can choose the tools we need for a particular task from platforms other than the ones that run the computer that you're typing on, and that's because we can put those operating systems in virtual containers and run many of them at the same time.

The amazing thing about Fusion is that it inherits the amazing talent from the virtualization leader, that is, VMware. VMware's ESXi hypervisor plus the management software, bundled as **vSphere**, as of this writing powers 98 percent of Fortune 500 enterprises' data centers (491 of 500, according to the corporate overview page on www.vmware.com). Businesses rely on this technology to run their entire operations 24/7, saving them tons of money not having to keep buying new hardware every time they need a server. They just spin up a virtual machine instead.

Fusion gets to inherit this enterprise-grade technology, bringing us the most stable and well-performing virtual platform on a Mac to date.

VMware Fusion has come a long way since the first few betas, with amazing features that I now can't live without.

In Version 5.0, we got to see some really great improvements, such as the following:

- Windows 8, Server 2012 support
- OS X Mountain Lion support, which includes AirPlay, Notification Center, and performance improvements with SSDs
- ESXi 5 support, which is great for testing VMware vSphere when combined with OVF file support
- Battery-saving enhancements
- Huge graphics performance improvements, such as the brand new OpenGL Linux graphics driver!
- User interface updates, which includes:
    - A new installer, making upgrades easier
    - An a-glance view of how much disk space your VMs are consuming
    - Built-in help via the Fusion Learning Center with videos
    - The **Take Snapshot** button can be put on the VM Toolbar, which is handy for quick snaps
    - Folders in the Library; great for those of us with many VMs
- Fusion Professional edition, which includes:
    - A custom network editor (finally!)
    - Large-scale enterprise deployment tools
    - Support for the OVF format for compatibility with VMware vSphere and VMware Workstation
    - The ability to create "restricted" virtual machines

In September 2013, VMware released VMware Fusion 6, and it further improved upon Version 5 that came before it.

The new version now supports the following:

- ▶ Mac OS X Mavericks, both as a Host OS and a VM (guest OS)
- ▶ Windows 8.1 support
- ▶ Retina Display support and better performance in every category

With Version 6, VMware Fusion is better than ever.

Fusion Professional, first introduced in Version 5, continues to be improved in Version 6. Fusion Professional is ideal for advanced users or in corporate environments because it allows for more security and prescriptive access to virtual machines than before. Admins can centrally manage and set time limits, disable access to USB devices, and enable guest disk encryption and passwords to prevent virtual machines from being changed.

There is also an advanced network editor so you can create complex multi-VM "virtual" networks, and it also supports "linked clones" for making a copy of a virtual machine that shares virtual disks with the parent virtual machine. Linked clones conserve disk space and allow multiple virtual machines to use the same basic software installation.

You can learn more about Fusion and Fusion Professional from the following links:

- ▶ `http://www.vmware.com/products/fusion/`
- ▶ `http://www.vmware.com/products/fusion-professional/`

Installing Windows 7 and upgrading to Windows 8 (Simple)

Unfortunately, Windows 8 and 8.1 are not easily available as non-upgrade `.iso` files. To use the tools provided by Microsoft, you actually need Windows to begin with. It's easy enough if you have bought a retail disk, but if not, you'll have to use Windows to create a bootable `.iso` file of Windows 8 anyway. In almost all cases, Microsoft expects you to already have Windows to go to Windows 8 or 8.1.

Further, more because not every application might be ready for Windows 8, to get the best of both worlds, what we'll do instead is essentially install both in such a way that we can switch between the two at will.

We'll do this by installing Windows 7 from the download of a clean-install ISO, taking a snapshot (or a linked clone if you're using Fusion Professional) and then upgrading it to Windows 8. You can even take another snapshot after Windows 8 has finished installing, upgrade to Windows 8.1, and have another point in time to go back to, or just go to Windows 8.1 without a second snapshot. The choice is yours, and it really depends on your needs.

If you have Fusion Professional, again, you can use the new linked clone feature instead of snapshots to conserve disk space.

Getting ready

To install Windows 8 in VMware Fusion, you'll need the following:

- ▶ An Apple Macintosh computer with VMware Fusion 6 installed
- ▶ 4 GB of RAM (8 GB or more recommended for native performance)
- ▶ 35 GB of hard disk space to complete the installation alone
- ▶ Recommended at least 50 GB of free space to accommodate the VM's natural growth
- ▶ Operating system installation media (disk or disk image) for Windows 7 and Windows 8

 Note that Microsoft Windows is obviously not included with VMware Fusion, but in this recipe, we will show you where to buy it.

How to do it...

For this recipe, we start with Windows 7 and then upgrade to Windows 8. We'll take a snapshot before upgrading to Windows 8 so that we can use Windows 7 when we need to.

You can download the Windows 7 "Trial" install image directly from the official Microsoft repository and save it to your Mac's `Downloads` folder, available at `http://msft.digitalrivercontent.net/win/X17-59186.iso`.

 Downloading the Windows 7 Trial `.iso` file from Microsoft (via Digital River) is legal and free of charge. Otherwise, you can use your Windows 7 Retail installation media.

For Windows 8, purchase the download directly from `www.microsoftstore.com` and access the download and the license key through your Microsoft Store account. It is quick and easy to get access to the download, and we'll do this within the same Windows 7 Trial virtual machine that we're about to create.

Since you should already have Fusion installed, let's get right to it.

Step 1 – installing Windows 7

Follow these steps:

1. The first thing to do is to launch VMware Fusion and create a new virtual machine using the Windows 7 Trial `.iso` file that we have downloaded from Microsoft, as shown in the following screenshot:

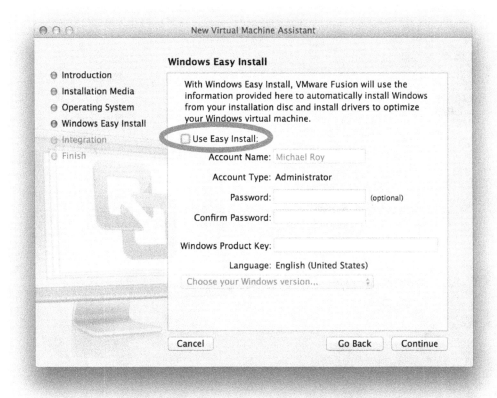

Walking through each of the steps to install Windows is beyond the scope of this book, but you can follow the process using the following resources:

- ❏ Creating a new virtual machine in Fusion from
  `http://kb.vmware.com/kb/1011677`

- ❏ Using the step-by-step process on my YouTube channel, available at
  `www.youtube.com/mikeroysoft`

2. Choose your Windows 7 `.iso` file or physical DVD with the **Choose a disk or disk image** button and choose **Windows 7 x64** as the **Operating System type**. If you use the download link I provided, the filename is `X17-59186.iso`.

3. Use the **Customize Settings** option to save the virtual machine and set the CPU and RAM settings before starting the installation. If your Mac has 8 GB or more of RAM and a quad-core CPU, to make Windows 8 perform at its best, I recommend setting the number of **Processors** to **2 processor cores** and setting the RAM to **4096 MB** (4 GB), as shown in the following screenshot. If your Mac has only 4 GB of RAM and a dual core CPU, assign 2048 MB (2 GB) of RAM and 1 processor core to the virtual machine.

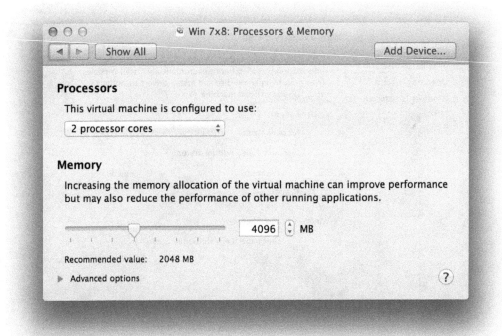

The reasoning is simple: give Windows enough resources to do the work it needs to do, but keep enough on the Mac to keep the rest of the computer running smoothly.

4. After you start the virtual machine for the first time, when the Windows 7 installer asks, perform the following steps:

    1. Create your username and password when prompted.

    2. *Do not* enter a license key. Make sure **Automatically activate windows when I'm online** is *unchecked*.

5. Let the installer complete. Once the installer has completed and you have access to the Windows 7 desktop, now is the time to take a snapshot.

6. Take a snapshot or a linked clone. We can later go back to this point in time and switch between using Windows 7 and Windows 8. We'll discuss this in detail in the *Much ado about snapshots (Intermediate)* recipe. To take a snapshot, simply click on the **Snapshots** button as shown in the following screenshot:

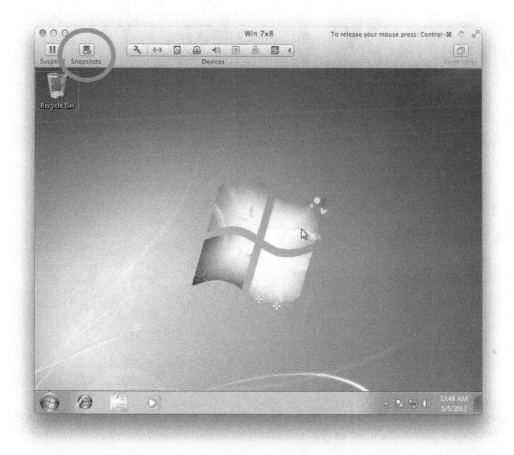

7. Now, click on the **Take** button, as shown in the following screenshot:

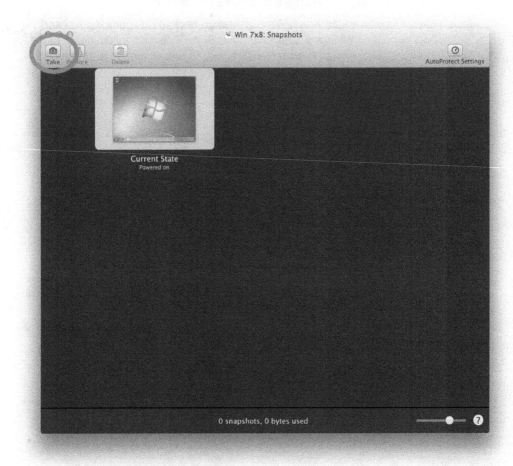

Windows 7 is installed, and we now have a snapshot; so, now we can go ahead and upgrade to Windows 8. Ultimately, if we want to use Windows 7, we'll need to license it. If you have a retail license for Windows 7, this is a perfect way to use it. If you have an OEM license (one that came with a PC), it might be better if you convert your existing PC, which is covered in a later recipe, and upgrade that to Windows 8 or 8.1.

We have seen what the **Snapshots** screen looks like. Taking a snapshot is as easy as a click of a button. Note that to take a linked clone, the virtual machine must be powered off and not suspended.

You can also take a linked clone if you are using Fusion Professional.

Attack of the clones

Clones are a new feature of Fusion 6 Professional, and work just like they do in VMware Workstation or vSphere, for those familiar with these platforms. There are two kinds of clones: linked clones and full clones.

A **linked clone** is a new virtual machine that uses an existing virtual machine as its "base image", also called a parent. It does not alter the original, but does read from it when it's running, so the original must be in the folder where it was when the linked clone was created. If it goes missing, the linked clone will not be able to start and will ask you to find the parent VM.

A **full clone** is a complete copy of a virtual machine, and does not require the original to be present. You can choose to preserve settings, such as IP address and MAC address, or have them given new properties at boot.

Clones are effectively treated as completely independent virtual machines; however, linked clones must be able to reach their parent virtual machine in order to work. They do not use the snapshot editor to be managed; however, each clone can even have its own independent snapshot tree using the snapshot editor.

Simply right-click on the virtual machine from the VM Library window and select **Create Linked Clone...**, as shown in the following screenshot:

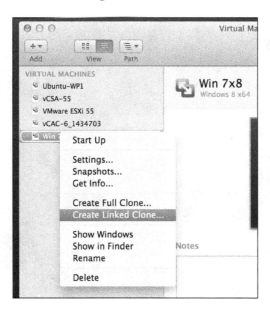

The clone shows up in the virtual machine library like any other virtual machine, and can even be running at the same time as its parent VM.

Step 2 – upgrading to Windows 8 or 8.1

Follow these steps:

1. Inside Windows 7, download and run the Windows 8 or 8.1 installer from your Microsoft Store account.

    To look up your order, obtain your license key and access the download. You can visit your account page at `www.microsoftstore.com`.

2. Run the `Windows 8 Setup.exe` installer from inside the virtual machine to upgrade your Windows 7 installation to Windows 8 or 8.1.

> You will require an active Internet connection to download the contents of the Windows 8 upgrade. The upgrade `.exe` file only contains the installer itself. **VMware Tools** is not required to be installed for a working Internet connection in Windows.

3. When prompted, enter your license key and begin the download process, as shown in the following screenshot:

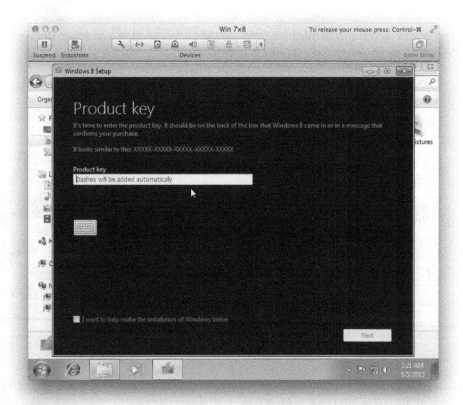

If you interrupt the process, it will resume when you start the installer again without having to re-enter the license key. Handy!

From here on, the rest of the installation is automated. So, just sit back and wait to personalize!

During the personalization process, I recommend customizing the installation as follows:

1. Turn on sharing.
2. Turn off Windows Update. (You could keep it on, but in a VM, it's best to do this manually.)
3. Turn all settings and other options off They may be OK for a desktop machine, but for a virtual machine, they're best left off.

Allow the installer to complete the upgrade. It may take some time depending on your Internet connection, as it's downloading the whole OS on the fly from Microsoft as it installs. The VM might also reboot once or twice, so just sit tight until everything is finished and you're at your shiny new Windows 8 desktop.

Once it resumes, it should come up as the Metro-UI-Laden Windows 8. Congratulations! the upgrade is nearly complete.

Step 3 – changing the OS type and installing/upgrading VMware Tools

Once the installer has finished and you've rebooted to the new Windows 8 desktop, power off the virtual machine and change the OS type to Windows 8 x64, as follows:

1. In the menu bar, click on **Virtual Machine** and click on **Shutdown**.
2. Navigate to **Settings | General**.
3. Click on **OS** and change it to **Windows 8 x64**. Click on **Change** when it prompts.
4. Close the **Settings** window and launch the VM by clicking on the big **Play** button.

When it finishes booting Windows 8, we can install or upgrade VMware Tools:

1. In the Mac menu bar, navigate to **Virtual Machine** | **Install VMware Tools** and select **Install** (if prompted). Windows will ask what to do about the D: drive, as shown in the following screenshot:

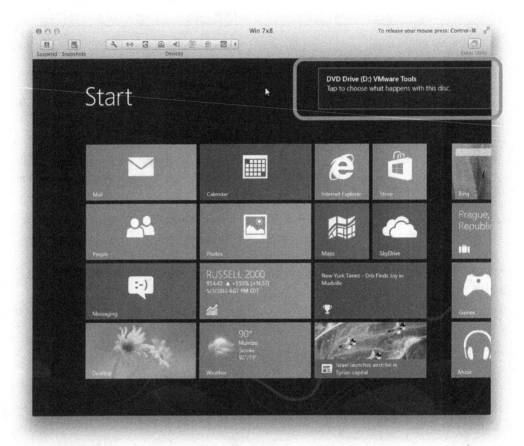

2. Windows will prompt for action. Click on **Run setup64.exe** as shown in the following screenshot:

3. Click on the **Typical** tools installer. The virtual machine will restart.

Once the VM restarts, Windows 8 is installed and ready to go!

At this point, you can also upgrade to Windows 8.1 by following the instructions available at http://windows.microsoft.com/en-us/windows-8/update-from-windows-8-tutorial.

Remember, you can take a snapshot (or a clone with Fusion Professional) now so that you can always go back to this fresh installation state, even after you upgrade to Windows 8.1!

You do not need to do anything special to the Windows 7 .iso files; they can be used as they are.

See also

▶ Windows 7 Professional English 64-bit available at `http://msft.digitalrivercontent.net/win/X17-59186.iso`

▶ Windows 8.1 Upgrade instructions available at `http://windows.microsoft.com/en-us/windows-8/update-from-windows-8-tutorial`

Keeping your old PC alive! (Intermediate)

Many users want to keep their ageing PCs alive on their new Mac hardware, and VMware Fusion is the perfect tool to do it. It's a great way to "upgrade your life" by getting a Mac, but still keep the tools that you are aware of. Here, we'll describe the steps you can take to clone your physical PC into a VMware Fusion virtual machine.

Getting ready

In order to migrate your PC, the PC must be connected to your home network. A wireless connection will take an extremely long time (I've seen *days*). It's recommended that you use a Gigabit Ethernet connection for both the Mac and the PC. You could also directly connect the Mac and the PC with an Ethernet cable and turn on **Internet Sharing** on the Mac by navigating to **System Preferences** | **Sharing**. This will allow the Mac and the PC to connect with each other without needing a router.

How to do it...

The process is pretty straightforward if you follow the wizard. To get started, make sure both your PC and Fusion are up and running. Both need to be connected to your network or to each other directly. Use Ethernet to connect everything for performance and stability.

Running the Migration Assistant

Follow these steps:

1. Within VMware Fusion, start the Migration Assistant by navigating to **File** | **Migrate Your PC...** and following the prompts. It will require that you download a small agent onto your PC and type a four digit security code created by it into the Migration Assistant, as shown in the following screenshot:

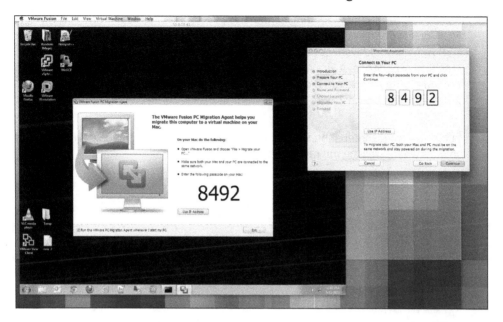

2. VMware Fusion provides an estimate of the time it could take to convert your machine. Once again, Ethernet is definitely recommended. In the previous screenshot, I am using Microsoft Remote Desktop for Mac (RDP) to connect to a computer in my lab and am about to start converting it over my Ethernet network.

   When running through the Migration Assistant, be sure to take note of how much space you have and how much is required to convert your PC.

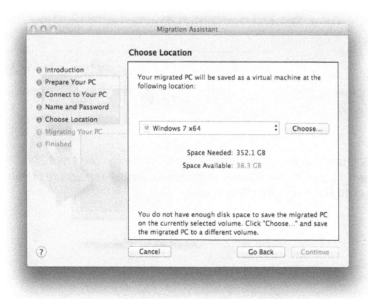

3. As you can see in the preceding screenshot, I don't have enough space on my MacBook Pro's main drive! So, I have to choose an external drive. A Thunderbolt or USB 3 drive would work best, as disk speeds need to be fast for an optimal virtual machine experience. A FireWire 800 drive is also adequate. We don't have to keep the VM on the Mac to run it or keep it in the virtual machine library; we just need to make sure the USB, FireWire, or Thunderbolt disk is connected when we want to run the VM.

In the following screenshot, we can see there is now enough space available on the volume where we'll be migrating the old PC:

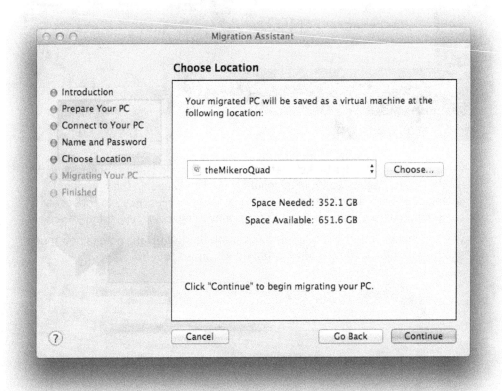

Remember, this process is going to take some time. In my example, I had 300 GB to convert, and I had to leave it running overnight. By comparison, a smaller machine of mine, which only consumed about 10 GB, took about 30 minutes.

How it works...

The process works because of the agent that was installed in the PC. Aside from just connecting the PC to the Fusion Migration Assistant with the four digit code, the agent copies the PC from the inside while it's running, and places the copy on your local Mac via the network. The fastest network connection would be using Gigabit Ethernet. Using Wi-Fi is not recommended. To compare, Wi-Fi (802.11n) usually pushes around 100-150 Mbps; Gigabit Ethernet, however, can hit 1000 Mbps. Plus, a large transfer like that over Wi-Fi is prone to interruption due to interference. Starting a 40-hour transfer all over again because someone turned the microwave on halfway through is certainly no fun!

There's more...

The Migration Assistant that comes with Fusion isn't the only way to convert your PC of course! Read on for other options.

More information

The VMware Fusion Migration Assistant is great because it's built on the enterprise-class VMware vCenter Converter. If for some reason the Migration Assistant doesn't work for you, or if you want to save your image to a disk because you only have Wi-Fi between your Mac and PC, you can use VMware vCenter Converter instead. vCenter Converter is free and gives you many more options when converting your PC to a virtual machine.

You can find VMware Converter and its documentation for download at:

- ▶ http://www.vmware.com/products/converter/
- ▶ http://www.vmware.com/go/getconverter

You can even use the Migration Assistant to transfer a virtual machine from another computer to Fusion. For example, if you had another Mac on your network and it had a VM running in Fusion, you could *copy* that VM by using the Migration Assistant in the same way. It would also work for VMs in Workstation, or even other hypervisors such as Xen, Hyper-V, VirtualBox, or even vSphere/ESXi. As long as Fusion can reach the Windows VM on the network, it should work.

Much ado about snapshots (Intermediate)

Snapshots are a fantastic feature of VMware Fusion because they allow you to *roll* the VM *back in time* to a previously saved state. Using snapshots is easy, but understanding how they work is important.

Now, first things first. A snapshot is *not* a backup, but rather a way to either safely roll back in time or to keep multiple configurations of an OS but share the same basic configuration. The latter is very handy when building websites. For example, you can have one snapshot with IE7, another with IE8, another with IE9, another with IE10, and so on.

A backup is a separate copy of the entire VM and/or its contents ("Your VM" and "Your Data") on a different disk or backup service. A snapshot is about rolling back in time on the same machine.

If you took the snapshot when we finished installing Windows 7 but before upgrading to Windows 8, you can easily switch back and forth between Windows 7 and 8 by simply restoring the state. Let's see how.

Getting ready

Firstly, the VM doesn't have to be running, but it can be. The snapshot feature is powerful enough to work even when the VM is still running, but goes much faster if the virtual machine is powered off or suspended. We can use the snapshot we took when we finished installing Windows 7. If you didn't take a snapshot at that time, you can go ahead and take a new snapshot now by clicking on the **Take** button from the snapshot window.

How to do it...

Snapshots are best taken when a VM is powered off. It doesn't have to be, but your computer will complete the "Take Snapshot" operation much faster if the VM is powered off or suspended. Both fully powered off and suspended tasks are much faster because the VM isn't in motion when the snapshot is taken, allowing the operation to finish at a single stroke. Otherwise, the way the snapshot mechanism works when a VM is running is that once it finishes, it has to now gather the new data that changed from when the snapshot operation started. So, if it took five minutes to take a snapshot, it then has to gather itself up to date for those five minutes. That might take a minute. After that, it has to go back again to gather that last minute. If that minute takes 20 seconds, it has to then gather those 20 seconds again. This is made worse with the more things you're doing within the virtual machine. So, get it done in one motion by suspending or powering off the VM first.

Launching the snapshot window and examining the tree

The following sequence of steps is used to initiate the snapshot process:

1. Click on the **Snapshots** button in the VM window and have a look at the snapshot interface. In my example, the following was the view of my "tree" right after we finished installing Windows 7:

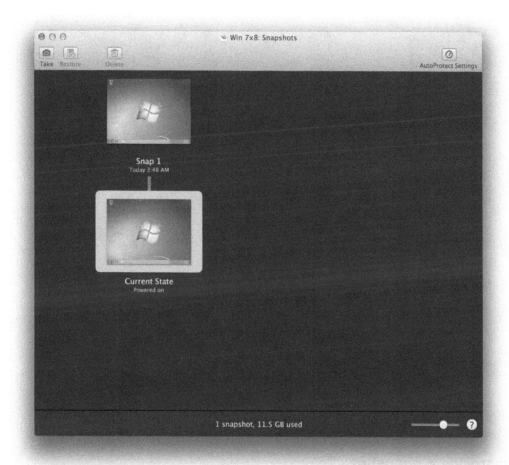

2. When I finished upgrading to Windows 8, I took another snapshot. This allows me to go back in time to both a fresh Windows 7 and Windows 8 installation, as shown in the following screenshot:

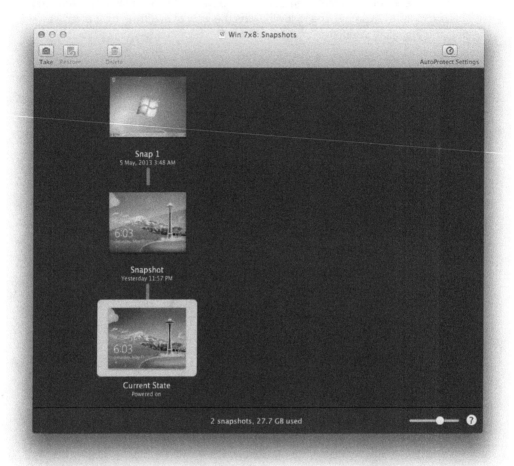

Restoring a snapshot

Having a TARDIS or DeLorean might be more fun, but for the rest of us, we can go back in time by restoring a snapshot. Let's go back to Windows 7 from our Windows 8 VM.

Follow these steps:

1. In the Snapshot Manager window, simply double-click on the base disk at the top of the tree to restore it. It will ask about saving the current state. Choose **Save** when prompted asks as shown in the following screenshot. You can rename the snapshot at any time from this window by right-clicking on the name and clicking on **Get Info**.

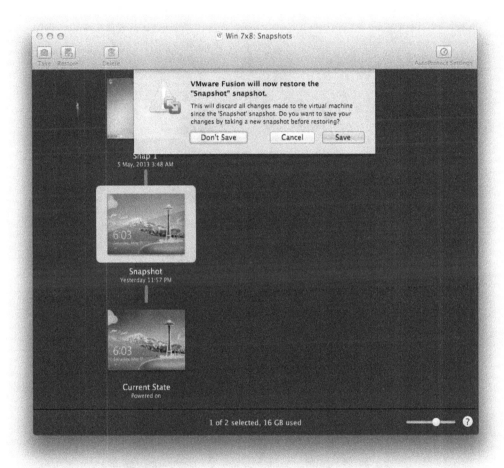

2. After a few seconds, depending on the speed of your Mac, the older version should now show as the **Current State**, as shown in the following screenshot. If the VM was running, it should just show up now as being Windows 7. If you see a spinning wheel in the upper-right corner, that's the "disk cleanup" activity working in the background. You can use the VM while it's doing this; however, it might be a bit slow on disk access while it's cleaning up the disks. If the VM is suspended or powered off when restoring, the operation is much faster because the VM isn't changing/running.

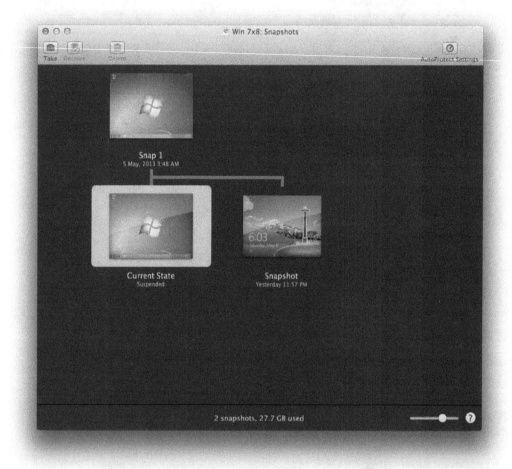

With this technique, you can switch between Windows 7 and Windows 8 with ease.

How it works...

In Fusion, all of the VM's files, are stored under **Documents | Virtual Machines** by default. Your C:\ drive in Windows is actually a series of files on the Mac named in sequence, with a .vmdk extension inside the Virtual Machines folder, as shown in the following screenshot. You can view the files by right-clicking on the VM and clicking on **Show Package Contents** from the Virtual Machines folder in the Finder.

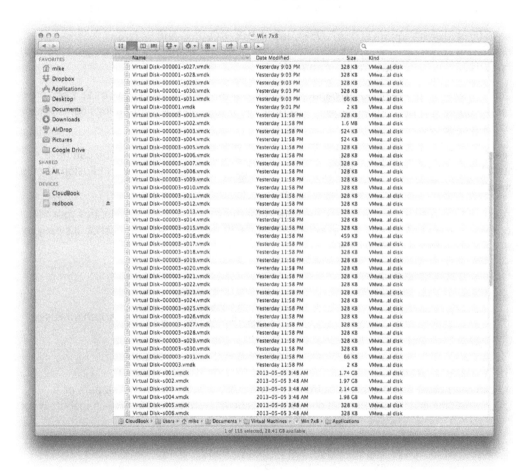

When you create a VM, it starts with one virtual disk (called the **base disk**). This virtual disk, or VMDK, is broken up into 2 GB "chunks" by default, but it can be one big chunk if desired. So, for a 20 GB disk, you end up with about 10 or 11 .vmdk files. This is for easy transport with drives that don't support large drives (such as MS-DOS/FAT32-formatted drives), and you may also have a performance benefit in certain cases.

When you take a snapshot, the currently active VMDK goes into read-only mode, and a new VMDK is created. All writes go to the new VMDK, and reads happen from the original VMDK when the bits are there. Fusion is smart enough to keep track of what files are where; so, when the VM is running, Fusion is reading all of the snapshots in the current state's chain.

A `.vmdk` file is thus named `<disk_name>-<snapshot_number>-<slice>.vmdk`.

So, in my example, `Virtual Disk` is my disk name. (I could have customized and specified something different by performing a Custom Virtual Machine operation at the beginning.)

I have three disks: `Virtual Disk`, `Virtual Disk-000001`, and `Virtual Disk-000003`. This means I have two snapshots and a base disk. (I took one snapshot and deleted it, which is why there's no `Virtual Disk-000002`).

Each of those disks are of 60 GB capacity, so there are 31 slices. (`s001` to `s031`). Each file starts around 300 KB and can grow to just over 2 GB. You can see where things can start to get confusing now.

It gets even better when you have snapshots that are based on snapshots. You can have multiple snapshots with a common parent, which introduces a new concept in Fusion, that is, **snapshot trees**.

Snapshots are also a great way to make sure something new isn't going to destroy your VM. So, if you are about to install some software that might be risky, take a snapshot. It's easy to roll back if something goes wrong.

There's more...

Snapshots are complicated, but there's great material out there by the gurus behind Fusion itself about how they work on a more technical level.

More information

You can read more about snapshots from Eric Tung, one of the original developers of Fusion (the blog is a bit old, but still completely accurate with respect to how snapshots work) at `http://blogs.vmware.com/teamfusion/2008/11/vmware-fusion-3.html`.

A great article by Eric to dispel some of the confusion around snapshots and how to use them is available at `http://blogs.vmware.com/teamfusion/2008/11/bonus-tip-snaps.html`.

One thing to note is that the more snapshots you have, the more effort the Mac has to make to "glue" them all together when you're running your virtual machine. As a rule of thumb, don't take snapshots and keep them around forever if you don't intend on rolling back to them regularly.

Also, each snapshot can grow to be the size of the entire `C:\` drive in Windows. Use them when necessary, but be aware of their performance and disk-usage costs.

Keeping Your VM and Your Data safe (Simple)

There are several options to protect your investment in Windows and Fusion, both within and outside of the VM. Snapshots, anti-virus, encryption, shared or mirrored folders, and backups are all great ways of keeping your data safe, but there are some considerations to be made when thinking about your VM's protection.

The way I see it, there are two main things that need protection: **Your VM** and **Your Data**.

Your VM means Windows system files and installed applications; the "virtual computer" itself, if you will. Your Data refers to the stuff inside Windows that matters most to you: your documents, files, pictures, and so on.

AutoProtect is a feature for automatically taking snapshots, so you don't have to think about it. You can also specify how many to keep on hand at a given time, as well as how often to take new snapshots.

AutoProtect is good in small doses. It causes a performance hit when the snapshot tree is too deep, relative to the speed of your hard disk. Most folks should disable this if they're experiencing performance issues. Using the methods I'll demonstrate, you can keep your data automatically protected without needing this feature. The AutoProtect feature settings are shown in the following screenshot:

VMware Fusion can also optionally encrypt the virtual disk, making the VM inaccessible from the Mac side in the event of someone stealing your Mac. In practical use, it makes it so you have to type a password every time the VM boots.

VM-level encryption, as shown in the following screenshot, is good if you really need to prevent someone else from accessing your data within Windows on your Mac, and it is catastrophic if you forget the password (your data is completely unrecoverable without it; that's the point!).

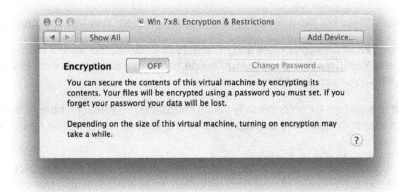

Most folks probably don't need this level of security, but if this specific type of data encryption is a requirement, Fusion obliges.

Time Machine backups are also important to consider because they work very well for normal files. Unfortunately, Time Machine treats .vmdk files like normal ones, and won't back up every file every time it runs (only the files that have changed). This means when it does take backups, the files end up being scattered across the entire history of the Time Machine drive, and therefore it is very difficult to put back together when something goes wrong.

So, Time Machine is good for Your Data and bad for Your VM, and it is therefore worth excluding Time Machine backups. This is done in your Mac's **Time Machine** feature in **System Preferences**, as shown in the following screenshot:

Finally, there are shared and mirrored folders, an amazing feature of Fusion.

In Windows, you have special virtual folders: Desktop, Documents, Downloads, Music, Movies, and Pictures. Your Mac has those folders too. Mirrored folders perform some magic to remap those "virtual folders" in Windows to a virtual network, shared from the Mac's equivalent folders. Plainly, it makes the Windows special folders *live* on the Mac instead of just inside your virtual machine (and its associated .vmdk files).

Personally, I prefer to mirror just my Documents folder. I save documents within Windows to the My Documents folder, and they end up in the Documents folder on the Mac. Then, Time Machine takes over and backs up the files just like they were normal files on the Mac (because, well, they are). This goes for things such as QuickBooks data, Office documents, Auto CAD files, and even video game save files.

With all these considerations, I present an approach which will keep both Your VM and Your Data safe without taking a performance or security hit.

Getting ready

To protect Your VM, the first thing to do is make sure your `Virtual Machines` folder is excluded from Time Machine backups. This is done by navigating to **System Preferences | Time Machine** on your Mac. Click on **Options** and then on **+** to add the `Virtual Machines` folder to be excluded, which is in the `Documents` folder. Fusion may have already set this for you when it was installing.

This of course means we must manually back up the VM, but that's the whole point. To do this, you'll need an external hard drive with sufficient free space. You can use your Time Machine drive (and indeed, I do), just not the Time Machine application itself.

To protect Your Data, we will use **Shared Folders** and **Mirrored Folders** to get your important data out of Windows where it can be safely backed up with Time Machine like the rest of the files on your Mac.

How to do it...

As we discussed earlier, there's Your VM and Your Data. Let's explore how to keep each of those safe independently.

Backup Your VM

As I mentioned earlier, your virtual machine is a series of files saved in your `Documents` folder, and it contains all of your Windows applications.

A good time to make a backup of Your VM is right after you've installed all of your applications and configured your user account the way you like it.

To do this, simply follow these steps:

1. Use Finder to navigate to `~/Documents/Virtual Machines`.

2. Select your virtual machine and copy it to your external hard drive by dragging-and-dropping it.

3. When you need to restore your virtual machine, you can either play the VM from your external hard drive by just double-clicking on it or you can drag it back to your `Virtual Machines` folder on your Mac.

Enabling Mirrored Folders

Now that Your VM is protected, let's protect Your Data.

Follow these steps:

1. Go to your virtual machine's **Settings** and click on **Sharing Settings**....

2. Click on the checkbox beside one of the folders you wish to mirror, as shown in the following screenshot:

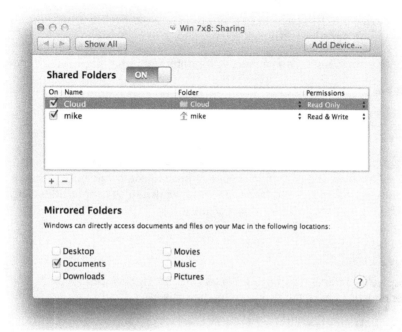

3. You can also click on **+** and add a different folder to share. In Windows, folders added here show up as the z: drive.

How it works...

With a backup of Your VM on an external drive and Your Data being backed up safely by Time Machine, you're now in a position to recover from just about any disaster.

Printing from Windows – how easy it is! (Simple)

Printing doesn't have to be hard, but there are a few things to consider when printing from a virtual machine on a Mac. Getting a printer going on a Mac is pretty easy, so the nice thing about Fusion is it extends that simplicity to your Windows VM. It does this through a feature appropriately called **Printer Sharing**. This feature automatically creates a virtual printer in Windows that only really *points* to the real printer installed on the Mac.

While the Printer Sharing feature is pretty simple to use, it doesn't do anything fancy, such as double-sided printing, duplexing, report ink level status, or any of the features you'd find in an All-In-One printer, such as a scanner.

Thankfully, there's more than one way to connect a printer to Windows, and you can take full advantage of the printer's full features if you need to.

There are three ways that you can connect your printer from your Mac to your Windows VM:

  ▶ The Printer Sharing feature
  ▶ USB pass-through
  ▶ Standard network printer setup

For standard printing, the built-in Printer Sharing feature is perfect. If you need to use the scanner part of an All-In-One printer, they need to be connected using USB pass-through. Printers that are connected to your Mac over the network can be connected directly, bypassing the Printer Sharing feature, so it can report on ink levels.

Getting ready

In this recipe, we'll go through setting up Printer Sharing, try USB pass-through, and connect to the printer directly from within Windows via the network.

How to do it...

With so many ways to print, let's look at how we can get the job done. Remember that you shouldn't use all of these methods, but pick one that works with your setup and stick with that. Once you're there, you can always switch to a different option, but just don't try to do more than one at a time, as they will conflict.

Option 1 – Printer Sharing

Printer Sharing should be enabled by default, but in case it's not in your VM's **Settings** window, you can add the shared printer with the following steps:

1. First, check if it's there and enabled by following these steps:
    1. From the virtual machine library, click on the virtual machine's **Settings** button.
    2. Click on **Printers**.
    3. Click on the checkbox that says **ON** as shown in the next screenshot:

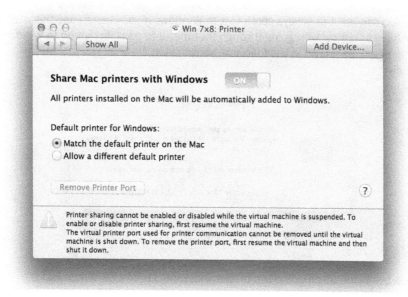

2.   If you don't have a **Printers** icon, you can add a new one by following these steps:

    1.   Click on the **Add Device...** button within the settings.

    2.   Click on **Printer**.

    3.   Click on **Add**.

Simple enough!

Option 2 – USB pass-through

Connecting to the printer directly via USB pass-through is essentially the same as plugging the printer directly into a physical Windows PC using a USB cable. Because Windows is virtual in our case, it means that you have to take the USB connection away from the Mac to give it to Windows. This means that you can only have the printer connected to either the Mac or Windows at one time, but not both.

To use USB pass-through, follow these steps:

1.   Click on the **Printer** icon from the bottom of the virtual machine window.

2.   Click on **Connect <your printer name>**.

Or, follow these steps:

1.   Click on the menu bar.

2.   Go to **Virtual Machine | USB**.

3.   Click on **Connect <your printer name>**.

However, when you plug the printer in via USB, Fusion will ask you what you want to do with the device. You can tell it to always connect it to Windows if you wish to use this method, and you'll never have to bother with going through that menu to pass it through to Windows from the Mac side again, as shown in the following screenshot:

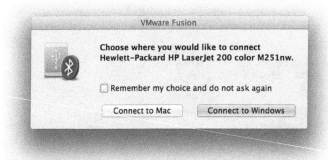

This action is the same as plugging the printer into a USB port on a Windows PC.

From here, standard Windows printer installation steps apply as directed by the printer manufacturer (installing drivers, software, and so on), as shown in the following screenshot:

Option 3 – network printer

If your printer happens to be a network printer with an Ethernet port or a wireless option, you can have the best of both worlds by just installing it the same way you would on a normal PC: as a network printer.

Remember that Printer Sharing only installs a printer proxy which looks like a regular printer in Windows, but in fact only connects to the currently installed Mac printer.

Connecting to the printer directly via the network gives you more control over your printer in Windows than Printer Sharing; so, it's great if you want to print to big, wide-output printers, 3D printers, vinyl printers, embroidery devices, futuristic sewing machines, and so on.

Ultimately, you do not need to use the built-in Printer Sharing feature in order to make your virtual machine print to any printer, so it really depends on what your needs are.

So, in this case, you would *not* plug the printer into the computer via USB. You would just install the printer, which is connected to your network (mine, for example, has both Wi-Fi and Ethernet options, and is a terrific little color laser printer!), the same way that you would if your virtual machine were a physical one.

Simple, right?

How it works...

Printer Sharing offers a very basic driver to Windows and allows you to print from both Windows and the Mac at the same time without changing any settings, but is limited in its capability.

Connecting directly via USB pass-through is the same as plugging the printer into a Windows PC with a USB cable, providing full functionality of the printer, but you can only connect it to either the Mac or Windows at one time, not both.

Connecting via the network is the best of both worlds if possible, providing both connections to the Mac and the Windows VM at the same time, while delivering full functionality to both.

Network adapters – what's the difference? (Simple)

One of Fusion's core components to make Windows worth using on a Mac is to provide it with some network connectivity. Considering there's only one wireless card on most Macs, with newer Macs having the option of a USB or Thunderbolt adapter for Ethernet, and with older ones that have built-in Ethernet, that network device needs to be shared with Windows, Fusion can't just take it away from the Mac like a USB device.

So, to solve the problem of absolutely needing the network adapter to only be connected to the Mac, the brilliant minds at VMware developed a virtual network adapter. This adapter is treated in Windows the same way as an NIC or network port on a desktop PC.

One thing VMware loves to give its users is choice; and with the network functionality built into Fusion, we are treated once again to some great choices.

You can share the network connection from the Mac to Windows or you can allow Windows to connect directly to the same network that the Mac does, or neither. Windows can be given a network adapter that can *only* connect to the Mac itself and nothing else, which is great for folks who are into software development or other sorts of testing where you want a network adapter in the VM, but don't want that VM to be on the physical network. For really restrictive scenarios, you don't even need a network adapter in the VM at all.

Getting ready

When I use my virtual machine, it's usually at my office. We have Wi-Fi, and that's fine for most of my tasks, but sometimes I need to do things on the corporate Intranet.

So, because I don't want all of my traffic to go through the corporate Intranet, I can set things up so that Windows uses it, but then set the interfaces on the Mac so that the Mac goes through the Wi-Fi first. Essentially, I now have Windows on Wi-Fi and Mac on Ethernet connecting to the corporate network. So, Internet Explorer can cruise the company SharePoint repositories and check stuff out with MS Word and MS PowerPoint (my favorites!), while Safari on the Mac side is blissfully cruising about the Internet at large.

So, as described, VMware Fusion provides three different types of network adapters. The adapter is what determines which sort of virtual network shows up in Windows.

The options are:

- ▶ NAT
- ▶ Bridged
- ▶ Custom, which includes Private to my Mac and custom networks created using Fusion Professional

In this recipe, we'll explore the different options and discuss when it's appropriate to use them.

How to do it...

You can always change these settings if something isn't working out with just a few quick clicks.

Option 1 – Internet Sharing/NAT

This is your standard **Internet Sharing** feature. It creates a virtual router, and that router provides the Windows VM with an IP address. It's exactly the same thing your wireless router at home does with your Mac.

I like to consider it as an Internet splitter as it shares one IP address with many devices. Using this mode, Windows may have issues accessing things that are on the network the Mac is connected to because of **Network Address Translation**, and if that's the case, you can use the **Bridged** method, as shown in the following screenshot:

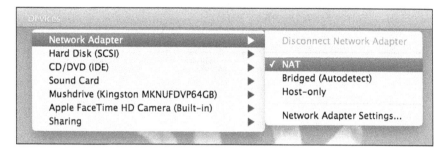

It's best to use NAT/Internet Sharing for general web surfing or Internet connectivity from Windows. If you really need Internet Explorer to browse the Internet, this is how I would do it.

In the following screenshot, using the Mac's **Activity Monitor** utility, we can see the **vmnet-natd** process running on the Mac side. This is what gives the Windows VM its "NAT" or "Shared" networking connection.

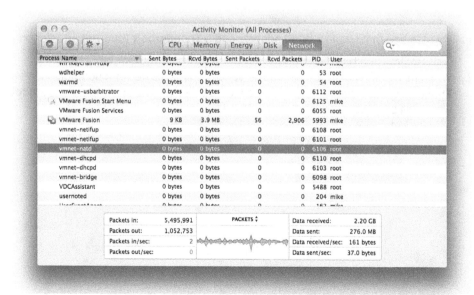

Option 2 – Bridged Networking

Bridged networking bypasses the NAT feature of Internet Sharing and instead allows you to connect directly through one of the available interfaces. Let's have a look at the following screenshot:

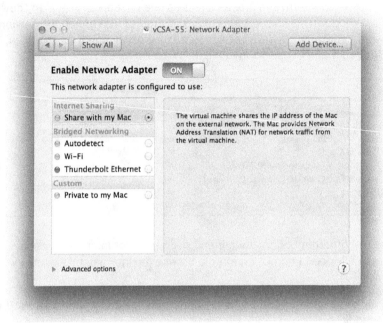

In this screenshot:

1. You can see that I have a **Wi-Fi** adapter and a **Thunderbolt Ethernet** adapter on my Mac (however, my Thunderbolt isn't connected right now, hence the red icon).

2. When using this mode, you can either specify a specific network adapter, such as my **Thunderbolt Ethernet** example I described earlier, or you can simply use **Autodetect**, which will pick the interface that the Mac is using to connect to the Internet.

3. If you want to make the Mac access one network and Windows another, you must set the **Service Order** in your Mac system preferences, as shown in the following screenshot:

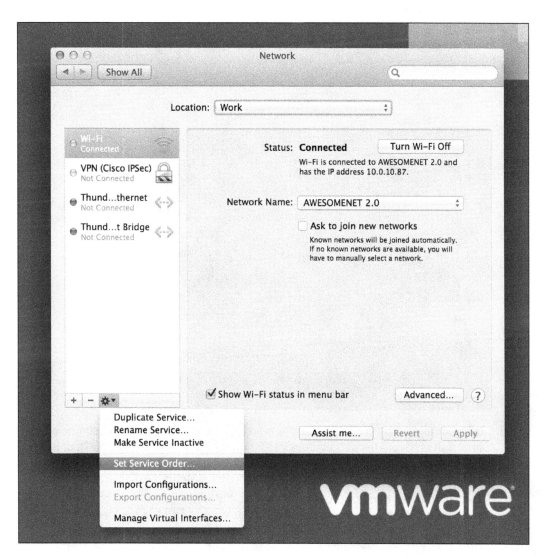

4. Set the option you want the Mac to use to be at the top. In my case, it's my VPN, followed by the Wi-Fi adapter that I want to give to the Mac, and the **Thunderbolt Ethernet** I'll put lower on the list and give it to Windows, as shown in the following screenshot:

5. Bridged Networking is best suited for corporate environments (but sometimes won't work if the network security is really high, in which case you must use NAT), or if you need to communicate with resources on the same network as the Mac (that is, network printers, scanners, other shared Windows systems, file servers, and so on).

6. Like I mentioned earlier, I prefer to get the best of both worlds. In my corporate environment, we have a Wi-Fi and an Ethernet setup, and while the Wi-Fi isn't as locked down, it also isn't connected to the corporate services (the ubiquitous "LAN"). The wired/Ethernet connection is on the LAN; however, its access to the Internet is limited for obvious security reasons.

7. So, as I described earlier, instead I plug a Thunderbolt Ethernet adapter into the Mac. I use Bridge Networking to my Windows VM (which in my case is a different VM provided by the company). I then set the network **Service Order** to have **Wi-Fi** at the top, so the Mac uses that first.

8. This way, my Windows machine is on the corporate LAN and I can access all the internal tools with it. (Hooray for SharePoint!) My Mac is on the Wi-Fi network, which has less restricted access to the Internet, so I can do all the research and communications that I need to using my Mac.

This gives me the best of both worlds, delivered through the power of VMware Fusion's advanced networking capabilities.

Option 3 – Private to my Mac in Custom

Custom networking provides the **Host Only** mode, as shown in the following screenshot, which prevents the Windows VM from connecting to anything but the Mac it's running on.

Custom networking in VMware Fusion Professional has the ability to define custom networks, whereby you can specify the details of the virtual network that Windows is given.

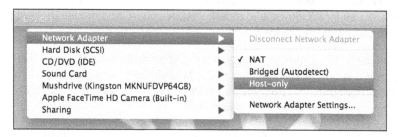

The best time to use Private to my Mac networking is if you must restrict your VM to only access the Mac itself and nothing else, including the Internet.

How it works...

With the three networking types, VMware Fusion can essentially act as a router or as a switch. A router provides Network Address Translation (NAT), and it can be thought of like a home router that "splits" one Internet connection to multiple computers (via Wi-Fi or Ethernet). Bridged networking turns Fusion into a switch, making it the same as if you had plugged in your Windows computer to the same thing your Mac was plugged into, putting them on the same network layer. **Host Only** is an isolated network type that is good for testing or when using a virtual machine that needs some networking, but can't be connected to the Internet. This is great if you build websites and want to test them in Windows but don't want to expose that machine to the Internet for security reasons.

Connecting peripherals to Windows – bringing the outside world in! (Simple)

We already talked about USB pass-through during our printer discussion, but it's worth noting that you can do much more than just pass printers through to Windows; you can pass just about any USB device that the Mac detects.

Your Mac has more to offer than just USB devices, however; there's a built-in **FaceTime** camera in all modern MacBook and MacBook Pro's, and there are also Bluetooth devices.

Also, while Fusion prevents this by default, you can even connect a keyboard and mouse to Windows via USB or Bluetooth. This is great in the following scenario: your Mac will be connected to two displays (or your MacBook will be connected to a secondary display), and you can have Windows on one screen with Mac on the other. You will have a dedicated keyboard and mouse for Windows, and a dedicated keyboard and mouse (or built-in keyboard and track-pad) connected to the Mac.

A word of caution on this... there's a reason it's not enabled by default! If you give Windows your only keyboard and mouse connected to the Mac via USB pass-through, you will take it completely away from the Mac, *trapping* you in Windows! Only use this if you have a second keyboard and mouse that you can dedicate to Windows.

You can even connect devices that don't normally work on a Mac into Windows, so long as the USB cable connecting it works and the device is picked up by the Mac.

Your Mac can detect a device even if it isn't designed to work on a Mac and lacks driver support (unless it or the USB cable is damaged of course). So, to reiterate, the device doesn't need to be supported on the Mac for it to be able to run in Windows. This is one of the really great reasons for using Fusion in the first place. You have some older hardware that only runs on Windows 95, so you put that in a virtual machine, plug your sewing machine into the Mac, and pass it on down to Windows.

I know I keep poking at the sewing machine, but believe it or not, that was a very popular use case with customers when I was in the Fusion Support team at VMware, and many of them only worked on Windows 95 or XP, so it makes for a great example. Folks used special "embroidery" software to make interesting patterns and then print to the sewing/embroidery machine. No Mac support? No problem!

Getting ready

In this recipe, we'll walk through connecting the FaceTime camera and an external keyboard to Windows. The keyboard process can be repeated to add a dedicated mouse if you wish; the process is the same, and the **modify VMX** step only needs to be completed once.

To do this, you'll obviously need an extra USB or Bluetooth keyboard and mouse, and a Mac with a FaceTime (or the older iSight) camera.

How to do it...

This is a pretty exciting recipe. Here, we'll show you how to have one computer behave completely like two independent computers; the Holy Grail of VMware Fusion's possibilities!

Connecting the FaceTime camera to Windows

Connecting the FaceTime camera is extremely simple, so we'll look at that first.
Follow these steps:

1. Make sure Windows is running.

2. Click on **Devices** from the Fusion window toolbar.

3. Click on **Apple FaceTime HD Camera (Built-In)**, as shown in the following screenshot (yours may read slightly different depending on your Mac model, I'm using a Mid 2012 Retina MacBook Pro). Or, from your Mac's menu bar, navigate to **Virtual Machine | USB & Bluetooth | Connect Apple FaceTime HD Camera (Built-In)**.

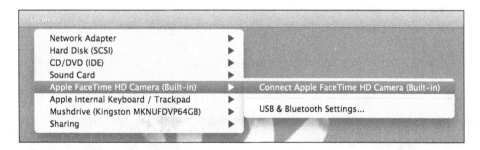

4. Windows now goes through a quick driver installation process. In Windows 8, it's fast and transparent. In the **PC Settings** window, however, it shows **Driver is unavailable**, as shown in the following screenshot, but that didn't prevent me from using the camera app or anything else that needed a webcam.

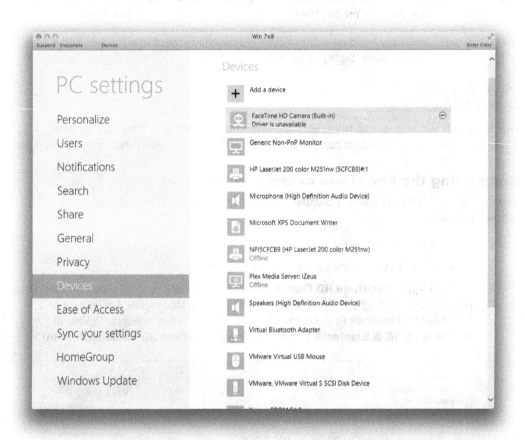

Dedicating an external keyboard exclusively to Windows (Advanced)

So, here's where we get a little crazy and risky. The idea here is to basically dedicate a keyboard exclusively to Windows, basically bypassing the Mac. I've mentioned this earlier, but don't do this unless you have a second keyboard! Otherwise, you will be completely stuck within Windows and you won't be able to get out and back to the Mac to do anything, including shutting down the machine! If you end up in this tragic state, your only recourse is to hold the power button until the Mac shuts off and reboots. Remember not to start Fusion until you change this VMX setting back!

Getting ready

What we're going to do is modify the virtual machine's configuration settings. Thanks to input from the Fusion Support team, we included a quick way to do this that doesn't involve having to dig through Finder to get to the VMX configuration file. You're welcome.

How to do it...

Firstly, make sure your virtual machine is powered off and not suspended!
It's important to do this first because **TextEdit** on Mac as of OS X 10.8 will save your file every time you change anything (you don't need to click on **Save** anymore), so it's not such a great idea to do this when a VM is actually running! You will likely break it if you do!
You have been warned!

Follow these steps:

1. We're going to follow KB 1014782 to modify the virtual machine's configuration file (the `.vmx` file), available at `http://kb.vmware.com/kb/1014782`.

2. In VMware Fusion, from the Apple menu bar, go to **Windows | Virtual Machine Library**.

 If your virtual machine is encrypted, you'll need to click on **Settings** and enter your password when prompted.

3. Hold the *option* key and right-click on the virtual machine. Select **Open Config File in Editor**.

4. Now that we have the configuration file open, we can go through VMware KB 1003418, available at `http://kb.vmware.com/kb/1003418`.

5. Scroll to the bottom and hit *return* a couple of times so it's easy for you to see the new configuration option.

6. Add the following lines to the very bottom:

```
usb.generic.allowHID = "TRUE"
usb.generic.allowLastHID = "TRUE"
```

7. Close TextEdit (it automatically saves the file).

8. Now, we should still have the virtual machine library window open from the earlier process. We can now launch the virtual machine with the new setting.

9. Once the virtual machine has finished booting, you can now pass a USB keyboard, mouse, or track-pad directly to it. To do this:

   1. Click on **Devices** from the toolbar.

   2. Click on **Connect Apple Keyboard**, as shown in the following screenshot:

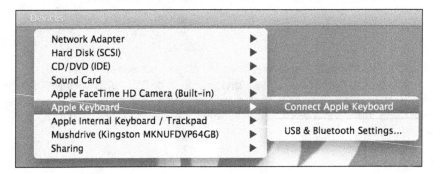

   3. In my case, I'm using a standard Apple USB keyboard; you can also use a Windows keyboard here, which is handy for folks who are more familiar with the layout when working within Windows.

   4. You can also go to the Apple menu bar and navigate to **Virtual Machine | USB & Bluetooth | Connect Apple Keyboard**.

And voila! Repeat this process for a mouse and you have yourself a whole computer-within-a-computer with an independent keyboard and mouse!

How it works...

The two main setups for this would look like the following:

▶ Keep Windows on the MacBook screen and Mac on an external monitor. You'd want to connect the internal Apple keyboard/track-pad, which will connect both of them at once.

▶ Keep Windows on an external display and Mac on the internal display. You'd connect a USB keyboard and mouse separately using the method I described earlier. Any Windows or Mac keyboard or mouse will do, but it's best to use USB.

The positioning of Windows is just a matter of dragging the Fusion toolbar where you want it and hitting the green button in the upper-left corner to fill the screen.

"I'm stuck, now what?" (Simple)

If you run into trouble, here's a great set of resources to look up.

Getting ready

To call VMware, it's good to have a My VMware account first. If you purchased Fusion directly from VMware, you're good. If you bought a box copy somewhere else, make sure you register your copy of Fusion at `my.vmware.com` before calling.

How to do it...

The following is a list of basic resources that you can use to help you get set up. These resources are also very handy in case you run into any issues while using the software:

1. Register VMware Fusion at `http://vmware.com/registernow`.

2. Go to VMware Fusion Community Forums at `http://communities.vmware.com/community/vmtn/fusion`.

3. Go to the VMware Fusion Resources at `http://vmware.com/go/fusionresources`.

4. View free support offerings for Fusion and Workstation, available at `http://www.vmware.com/support/services/complimentary.html`.

5. Call VMware directly at **1-877-486-9273 (1-877-4-VMware)**.

Summary

Using VMware Fusion is pretty awesome once you get the hang of it. It has a lot of fantastic features that work great in different situations, but it's not always obvious when to use which setting or why. I hope this book has been able to give you a better understanding of when to use the different options available to you, and ultimately leads you to becoming a VMware Fusion power user!

Let's recap some of the points covered in this book to make sure they stick:

- **Performance**:
  - Give Windows no more CPU and RAM than it needs, but no less either. If you're unsure, just split it down the middle. The idea is to leave enough for the Mac to run the computer and enough for Windows to run Windows.
  - Don't take too many snapshots. More than two or three will seriously degrade performance, especially on computers without solid state drives (SSDs).

- ❏ Disable AutoProtect unless you know you need it, for example, if you are the type that always break things and need a constant roll back point, and can live with the performance penalty (you know who you are!). If you have a modern Mac with an SSD, it's not that noticeable a performance hit. If you have an older one with a standard hard drive, you should avoid this feature.

► **Security**:

- ❏ Encrypt your VM for maximum security from anyone who could get physical access to your system, but don't lose that password!
- ❏ Keep a backup of Your VM separate from Your Data.
- ❏ Use Shared and Mirrored Folders, and Time Machine to keep Your Data safe.
- ❏ Keep a copy of Your VM on an external drive just in case. (When it boots, tell it that you moved it, so it doesn't change the MAC address and Windows doesn't know that it's been copied).

► **Productivity**:

- ❏ Keep Windows 7 and Windows 8 on the same VM using a snapshot. Remember not to have too many, but this is great if you need to go back to something in Windows 7 that isn't compatible with Windows 8.
- ❏ Remember to use only one printing method at a time.
- ❏ Connect a FaceTime camera to Windows to use it there.
- ❏ If you have to, connect a USB keyboard and mouse directly to Fusion. This is really only necessary if you want to dedicate a Windows keyboard to Windows only.
- ❏ Remember to call VMware's excellent support folks to get help when you need it. One of the benefits of paying for Fusion is that it comes with free e-mail support! If you need an extra hand, you can pay a small fee and they can give you a call to talk in person, and even remote-control your Mac to show you exactly what needs to be done to solve even the most complex of problems.

 **Thank you for buying**
Instant Getting Started with VMware Fusion

About Packt Publishing

Packt, pronounced 'packed', published its first book "*Mastering phpMyAdmin for Effective MySQL Management*" in April 2004 and subsequently continued to specialize in publishing highly focused books on specific technologies and solutions.

Our books and publications share the experiences of your fellow IT professionals in adapting and customizing today's systems, applications, and frameworks. Our solution based books give you the knowledge and power to customize the software and technologies you're using to get the job done. Packt books are more specific and less general than the IT books you have seen in the past. Our unique business model allows us to bring you more focused information, giving you more of what you need to know, and less of what you don't.

Packt is a modern, yet unique publishing company, which focuses on producing quality, cutting-edge books for communities of developers, administrators, and newbies alike. For more information, please visit our website: www.packtpub.com.

Writing for Packt

We welcome all inquiries from people who are interested in authoring. Book proposals should be sent to author@packtpub.com. If your book idea is still at an early stage and you would like to discuss it first before writing a formal book proposal, contact us; one of our commissioning editors will get in touch with you.

We're not just looking for published authors; if you have strong technical skills but no writing experience, our experienced editors can help you develop a writing career, or simply get some additional reward for your expertise.

Instant VMware Player for Virtualization

ISBN: 978-1-84968-984-7   Paperback: 84 pages

A simple approach towards learning virtualization to play with virtual machines

1. Learn something new in an Instant! A short, fast, focused guide delivering immediate results.

2. Discover the latest features of VMware Player 5.0.

3. Evaluate new technology without paying for additional hardware costs.

4. Test your applications in an isolated environment.

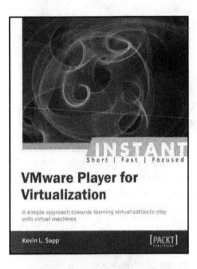

Implementing VMware vCenter Server

ISBN: 978-1-84968-998-4   Paperback: 324 pages

A practical guide for deploying and using VMware vCenter, suitable for IT professionals

1. Gain in-depth knowledge of the VMware vCenter features, requirements, and deployment process.

2. Manage hosts, virtual machines, and learn storage management in VMware vCenter server.

3. Overview of VMware vCenter Operations Manager and VMware vCenter Orchestrator.

Please check **www.PacktPub.com** for information on our titles

VMware vSphere 5.x Datacenter Design Cookbook

Over 70 recipes to design a virtual datacenter for performance, availability, manageability, and recoverability with VMware vSphere 5.x

Hersey Cartwright

[PACKT] enterprise

VMware vSphere 5.x Datacenter Design Cookbook

ISBN: 978-1-78217-700-5   Paperback: 260 pages

Over 70 recipes to design a virtual datacenter for performance, availability, manageability, and recoverability with VMware vSphere 5.x

1. Innovative recipes, offering numerous practical solutions when designing virtualized datacenters.

2. Identify the design factors—requirements, assumptions, constraints, and risks—by conducting stakeholder interviews and performing technical assessments.

3. Increase and guarantee performance, availability, and workload efficiency with practical steps and design considerations.

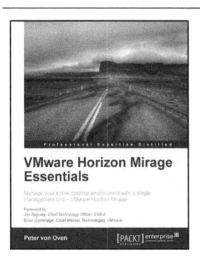

VMware Horizon Mirage Essentials

Manage your entire desktop environment with a single management tool – VMware Horizon Mirage

Foreword by
Joe Baguley, Chief Technology Officer, EMEA
Brian Gammage, Chief Market Technologist, VMware

Peter von Oven

[PACKT] enterprise

VMware Horizon Mirage Essentials

ISBN: 978-1-78217-235-2   Paperback: 166 pages

Manage your entire desktop environment with a single management tool–VMware Horizon Mirage

1. Deliver a centralized Windows image management solution for physical, virtual, and BYOD.

2. Migrate seamlessly to new versions of operating systems with minimal user downtime.

3. Easy-to-follow, step-by-step guide on how to deploy and work with the technology.

Please check **www.PacktPub.com** for information on our titles